Especially for:

••

From:

••

Date:

••

Our mission is to publish and distribute inspirational products offering exceptional value and biblical encouragement to the masses.

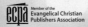
Member of the
Evangelical Christian
Publishers Association

Printed in China.

Our
Family
Christmas

An Advent Devotional

Karon Phillips Goodman

BARBOUR
PUBLISHING

Contents

> *"I believe that you are the Messiah,
> the Son of God, who is to come into the world."*
> JOHN 11:27 NIV

Because *Christ our Savior was born on Christmas Day*, our world was forever changed. The *wondrous gift* God gave us became the source of every wondrous gift to follow, and we have the Christmas season in which to hold our family close in *comfort and joy* and inspire us throughout the year to return *our finest gifts* to Him.

The Christmas story is an old story, but its power and purity remind us of the greatest and deepest love and sacrifice of our Father. One *silent night* in a town called Bethlehem, *Christ is born of Mary*. God's gift of His everlasting love came to us in flesh and stays in Spirit, our Immanuel Promise always guiding us and accepting our humble efforts to serve with Him.

When our *hearts prepare Him room*, we fear not the world we don't understand, but trust instead *the angel voices* still as true as *the night when Christ was born*. And we have the blessed opportunity to *go tell it on the mountain* in our lives to all who will hear of *Jesus, Lord at thy birth*, because the best thing to do with every priceless gift is to share it.

The sharing of the gift of Jesus begins in our homes, with those we love the most. We rejoice in the faithful reminder of His love and grace, *goodness and light*. We pause for this yearly booster shot of celebration because He is Lord of lords and King of kings, the gift we both share and receive with each breath because He lives. It's *peace on earth* to spend special moments with our family during this special season. *Let us adore Him* together.

Let us see beyond the wrapping paper and blinking lights to the everyday opportunities to bring *glory to our newborn King*, through all we say and do in kindness and generosity, faith and love. He's waiting for us to see past presents and dinners to the significance of *the first Noel*, waiting for us to live boldly the message and spirit of Christmas and do our part to deliver *goodwill to men* everywhere.

And we learn best when we're teaching those who depend on us the most. So for a few moments these next few days, in the *light of a star sweetly gleaming* and with those we love, let us remember this gift of *joy to the world*.

Do you hear what I hear? That's God's whisper of love in the gift of Christ, when *away in a manger*, dark and quiet, the *Son of God, love's pure light*, is born of Mary and given to us.

Do you see what I see? Each reading and activity here is to accompany you and your family through this blessed season. May your memories of this experience of *wondering love* return the joy of the gift of Jesus to you and your family on Christmas and always—because Christmas is a message that lasts a lifetime, ours and His. *Rejoice!*

> *Joy, joy, for Christ is born,*
> *The Babe, the Son of Mary!*

NOVEMBER 28
Receiving and Giving

In the sixth month of Elizabeth's pregnancy, God sent the angel Gabriel to Nazareth, a town in Galilee, to a virgin pledged to be married to a man named Joseph, a descendant of David. The virgin's name was Mary. The angel went to her and said, "Greetings, you who are highly favored! The Lord is with you." Mary was greatly troubled at his words and wondered what kind of greeting this might be. But the angel said to her, "Do not be afraid, Mary; you have found favor with God. You will conceive and give birth to a son, and you are to call him Jesus."

LUKE 1:26- 31 NIV

God gave His gift of pure love by allowing one of us to carry out His plan. Yes, Mary's character was impeccable and her willingness to serve greatly honorable, but perhaps what God saw most when He looked at His "highly favored" daughter was the depth of her love, pure as God's and out there for everyone to see. She chose to give the gift that only she could—bearing our Savior.

At Christmas and always, we learn from Mary how to live out loud our love for God. We can grab onto whatever God places before us and live a life that says, "God gives, I receive, and then I give back. *Watch!*"

Today we can touch our family members, friends, and even strangers with the simple and pure love of Christ. We can do what Mary did—trust that God has found something favorable within *us* that fits the special work He has for us. And because He loves with a pure love that supplies whatever we lack, we can live our love for Him out loud simply by doing what He asks. That's a gift we both receive from God and can return to Him at will and without fear. Because God still gives and receives, so can we.

Prayer

Father, thank You for the opportunity to follow Mary's example and love You out loud to those around us.

Activity

Help your children understand how simple loving God is—receiving His grace, following Him, and showing Him to others. As a family, decorate a greeting card for a faraway friend or put together a basket of candy for a lonely neighbor. Younger children may enjoy calling a family member on the phone and singing a carol. Remind your children that God is especially pleased when we love Him by loving others.

O Holy Night

O holy night, the stars are brightly shining;
It is the night of the dear Savior's birth!
Long lay the world in sin and error pining,
Till He appeared and the soul felt its worth.
A thrill of hope, the weary soul rejoices,
For yonder breaks a new and glorious morn.
Fall on your knees, O hear the angel voices!
O night divine, O night when Christ was born!
O night, O holy night, O night divine!

Truly He taught us to love one another;
His law is love and His Gospel is peace.
Chains shall He break for the slave is our brother
And in His name all oppression shall cease.
Sweet hymns of joy in grateful chorus raise we,
Let all within us praise His holy name!
Christ is the Lord! O praise His name forever!
His pow'r and glory evermore proclaim!
His pow'r and glory evermore proclaim!

A Crown for Jesus

"He will be great and will be called the Son of the Most High; and the Lord God will give Him the throne of His father David; and He will reign over the house of Jacob forever, and His kingdom will have no end."
LUKE 1:32–33 NASB

Jesus, who always was and always will be, makes His debut in human form one holy night—and the world is forever changed. The Babe born to live and die and live again is the ultimate circle, and His divinity and sovereignty reign forever in our hearts and in our world.

Christmas reminds us again of His eternal love and unshakable grasp on our lives. Gabriel was clear in His announcement so that we can be clear in our understanding—as constant as God's breath on the leaves of the trees and steady as His hand shoving waves to the shore, Jesus' living presence encircles us and makes Christmas live eternally in our hearts.

Part of our Christmas joy, and our every-other-day joy, too, comes in partnering with Jesus in His reign. He leads and we follow, to touch those we meet with a hand of friendship, a gift of forgiveness, the grace of understanding.

He is Son of the Most High—and because of His love, we become part of His kingdom. Because of His will, we become part of His reach to those around us. Before He was born of flesh, God created Him to meet our needs—and with Him we'll serve others, doing all we can to be the physical evidence of His unbroken love. It's our honor to share the gift of Christmas every day, never ending.

Prayer

Father, thank You for King Jesus who reigns over our whole world and our family, now and forever, and lets us serve with Him.

Activity

Make a crown with your children out of construction paper, craft sticks, pipe cleaners, or whatever you have. Use it for a tree topper, a table centerpiece, or package decoration. Explain to your children that Jesus' love is like the circle of a crown—no beginning and no end because it always was and always will be. His love and power last forever because God made Him that way.

Silent Night

Silent night, holy night,
All is calm, all is bright
Round yon virgin mother and Child.
Holy Infant, so tender and mild,
Sleep in heavenly peace,
Sleep in heavenly peace.

Silent night, holy night,
Shepherds quake at the sight;
Glories stream from heaven afar,
Heavenly hosts sing Alleluia!
Christ the Savior is born,
Christ the Savior is born!

Silent night, holy night,
Son of God, love's pure light;
Radiant beams from Thy holy face
With the dawn of redeeming grace,
Jesus, Lord, at Thy birth,
Jesus, Lord, at Thy birth.

Silent night, holy night,
Wondrous star, lend thy light;
With the angels let us sing,
Alleluia to our King;
Christ the Savior is born,
Christ the Savior is born!

Who Do You Trust?

This is how the birth of Jesus the Messiah came about:
His mother Mary was pledged to be married to Joseph,
but before they came together, she was found to be pregnant
through the Holy Spirit. Because Joseph her husband was
faithful to the law and yet did not want to expose her to
public disgrace, he had in mind to divorce her quietly.
MATTHEW 1:18–19 NIV

We can understand Joseph's concern, surprised by Mary's news of the Christ child's coming. Those around him might not believe Mary about her visit from the angel, and the best choice might seem to leave her quietly without facing the public doubt about the impending birth. But Joseph wasn't sure. . . .

Sometimes we're faced with situations that pit us against what we believe and what the world might believe about us. That's when we remember the value of those who have always been honest with us and the value of our own honesty, too.

Mary's character made her a credible source of information. It's important that we work to build that same credibility with those around us every day. We do that by telling the truth, by being a good representative of Christ in all we do, by following through on our promises to those we love.

Family members learn to trust each other and friends learn to trust friends over time—it's a deeply satisfying gift from God. And we learn to be trustworthy because Jesus showed us how. He has never lied to us, abandoned us, tricked us, or led us the wrong way. Let us always value our trusted relationships and work every day to make them even better, especially at Christmas.

Prayer

Father, thank You for the gift of trust to share with each other and Christ. Please help us live all our relationships in trust.

Activity

Show your children several sets of two photos, one of a parent and one of a stranger, then one of a grandparent and one of a stranger, etc. Ask which person in each set of photos they would trust. Then do a simple exercise, such as close your eyes and tell a child that you trust her to give you a kiss on the cheek and explain that by being trustworthy in small areas, we gain trustworthiness in bigger ones.

Good King Wenceslas

Good King Wenceslas looked
out on the Feast of Stephen,
When the snow lay round about,
deep and crisp and even.
Brightly shone the moon that night,
though the frost was cruel,
When a poor man came in sight,
gathering winter fuel.

Hither, page, and stand by me,
if you know it, telling,
Yonder peasant, who is he?
Where and what his dwelling?
Sire, he lives a good league hence,
underneath the mountain,
Right against the forest fence,
by Saint Agnes' fountain.
Bring me food and bring me wine,
bring me pine logs hither,
You and I will see him dine,
when we bear them thither.
Page and monarch, forth they went,
forth they went together,
Through the cold wind's wild lament
and the bitter weather.

DECEMBER 1
His Faithful Guidance

But after he had considered this, an angel of the Lord
appeared to him in a dream and said, "Joseph son of
David, do not be afraid to take Mary home as your wife,
because what is conceived in her is from the Holy Spirit.
She will give birth to a son, and you are to give him the
name Jesus, because he will save his people from their sins."
MATTHEW 1:20–21 NIV

$\mathcal{E}$ager to help Joseph make his decision about marrying Mary, God chose to reveal His will in a dream. He may lead us the same way today—or, more often, He'll guide us with His Word, the teachings of Jesus, and the blessing of wisdom we acquire the more we learn about Him. It's His beautiful and strong gift of guidance that grows the more we rely on it.

Faithful as the earth's travels, God continues to reveal Himself to us through the simple and, especially, the scary times of our lives—allowing us to know Him better so that we'll hear His voice and learn to trust His will more securely every day, even without an angel in a dream. God showed us how Joseph trusted and followed Him so that we can, too.

May we always remember the gift of Christ, God's guiding Word come to life. May we study and cherish God's Word and humbly accept His guidance so that we'll know when He speaks to us. Trusting the Giver to impart to us no less than the best answer and the best route, we can put our feet in the prints He leaves in every moment and mix-up in our lives. We can go on to our great and unique purposes when we go with God. Christmas is our time to begin, or begin again, our reliance on this special gift of His guidance.

Prayer

Father, thank You for guiding us and helping us trust You as Joseph did.

Activity

For your family Bible or each child's Bible, make covers that say something like "Our Answers" or "The Gift of Guidance" and reinforce to your children how God's Word and the teachings of Jesus will always lead them and help them make good choices. Decorate the covers and place the Bibles under your Christmas tree or in another place of honor for the season.

Go, Tell It on the Mountain

Go, tell it on the mountain,
Over the hills and everywhere
Go, tell it on the mountain,
That Jesus Christ is born.

While shepherds kept their watching
O'er silent flocks by night
Behold throughout the heavens
There shone a holy light.

The shepherds feared and trembled,
When lo! above the earth,
Rang out the angel chorus
That hailed the Savior's birth.

Down in a lowly manger
The humble Christ was born
And God sent us salvation
That blessed Christmas morn.

For to us a child is born, to us a son is given,
and the government will be on his shoulders.
And he will be called Wonderful Counselor,
Mighty God, Everlasting Father, Prince of Peace.
ISAIAH 9:6 NIV

$\mathcal{I}$saiah prophesied years before Jesus' physical birth, centuries before mere mortals could touch Him and see Him, millennia before our own Christmas celebrations—and it's all come true. Before computers could read and microwaves could cook, He was. And He always will be. That reminder comes again at Christmas each year—and when the security in our lives can feel as transient as a stock market's gains, the promise of His everlasting being is reassurance we grab onto and don't let go.

The Everlasting Father who lives in our hearts takes on the fears and trials of this life that only *feel* everlasting—the jagged struggles that bounce off our raw and bleeding hearts and threaten to knock us down, shatter our focus, and leave us whimpering and beat. But unlike Isaiah's listeners, we don't have to wait for our Wonderful Counselor to appear. He came to earth with Christmas and stays to love us always.

We trust Jesus is alive in our hearts, we see Him in the kindness of strangers, and we feel Him in the love of our family members. He is everywhere at once because we all need Him, and Christmas reminds us again that our Jesus will outlast everything—and knowing that, we know all we need to know.

Prayer

Father, thank You for our everlasting Jesus and His love and grace that never end.

Activity

Help your children understand the difference between things that are everlasting and things that aren't. Let each child name something that doesn't last—a movie, a tummy ache, a birthday cake, a flower, a scratch or bruise—these aren't everlasting. But a parent's love and our Father's love are, and no matter what, no matter where, Jesus lives and loves us forever.

O Come, O Come, Emmanuel

O come, Thou Wisdom from on high,
Who orderest all things mightily;
To us the path of knowledge show,
And teach us in her ways to go.

Rejoice! Rejoice! Emmanuel
Shall come to thee, O Israel.

O come, Thou Rod of Jesse, free
Thine own from Satan's tyranny;
From depths of hell Thy people save,
And give them victory over the grave.

Rejoice! Rejoice! Emmanuel
Shall come to thee, O Israel.

DECEMBER 3
Present, Now and Forever

*So all this was done that it might
be fulfilled which was spoken
by the Lord through the prophet,
saying: "Behold, the virgin
shall be with child, and bear a Son,
and they shall call His name Immanuel,"
which is translated, "God with us."*
MATTHEW 1:22–23 NKJV

If God is with us in Jesus (and He is), then it follows that we're with Him. Let us not overlook His beautiful and generous gift of abiding with us, so much more than sharing the same space. God's gift of abiding means sharing our lives and making us a vessel to receive and pass on His grace and peace and courage and wisdom and love. It means we can be more like Him every day because He gives us Himself.

Our Father knows our flaws and shortcomings, but He loves us more than we can mess up. And so each Christmas we're reminded of His ability to do anything but turn away from us. We joyously celebrate our "God with us" Savior's birth because the gift never ends.

Though steady stars may be obscured by passing clouds, they are no less present and powerful. And even when we feel momentarily alone and alarmed by passing fears, our Immanuel gift is no less present and powerful. Christmas tells us that from one silent night to a forever future, we abide with the One who came for us and will not leave. And close in heart, we learn to be like Him, sharing grace and peace and courage and wisdom and love because He first gave it all to us.

Prayer

Father, thank You for Your greatest Gift, our Savior Jesus Christ, who abides with us. Please help us be more like You in every way, every day.

Activity

For each family member, draw and cut out a small heart from construction paper or a greeting card. Write on each one "God is with me" or "My Immanuel gift" or something similar. Be sure family members will have their hearts with them each day, in a wallet, lunchbox, favorite book, or other item. Remind your children that Jesus is always with them and Christmas is a beautiful time to remember and celebrate that gift of abiding even more.

O Little Town of Bethlehem

O holy Child of Bethlehem,
descend to us, we pray;
Cast out our sin, and enter in,
be born in us today.

We hear the Christmas angels
The great glad tidings tell
O, come to us, abide with us
Our Lord, Emmanuel
Our Lord, Emmanuel

DECEMBER 4
Active Rest

* * *

"For nothing will be impossible with God."
LUKE 1:37 NASB

The angel Gabriel reassures Mary that what appears quite impossible to her is simply a matter of will for God. And the reassurance continues for us today, because when we practice our trust, we can make Gabriel's statement ourselves in total confidence and rest. And that rest is a wonderful gift from God.

The gift of rest comes when we trust what we can't see because we trust that He sees us, and that's enough. And if that's true and possible, no confines will ever hold His will. We trust unseen and believe the Immanuel promise of "God with us"—the most important and impossible-looking blessing of all, that gives us rest like nothing else.

But this rest is no lazy or bored time of inactivity—no, it's just the opposite, because it means we're able to enjoy our lives and our families and all God's planned for us because we trust God has everything in His hands and knows exactly what He's doing with it all and with us every minute. We can dare to dream great dreams and follow the directions He gives us. We can do our part like Mary did and leave everything else to Him—and worry not one bit but rest instead, knowing our Father is in control, seeing all we can't and seeing us without fail. It's Christmas every day.

Prayer

Father, thank You for the opportunity to rest in our trust of Jesus who is always able to do the impossible because of who He is.

Activity

Help your children understand God's unlimited possibilities. Can you see inside a Christmas present? No, but God can. Can you listen to everyone's prayers at one time? No, but God can. Encourage your children to give their own examples of something they or a family member can't do but God can.

Behold the Great Creator Makes

Behold the great Creator makes
Himself a house of clay,
A robe of virgin flesh He takes
Which He will wear for ay.
Hark, hark, the wise eternal Word,
Like a weak infant cries!
In form of servant is the Lord,
And God in cradles lies.

This wonder struck the world amazed,
It shook the starry frame;
Squadrons of spirits stood and gazed,
Then down in troops they came.
Glad shepherds ran to view this sight;
A choir of angels sings,
And eastern sages with delight
Adore this King of kings.

DECEMBER 5
Worshipful Serving

And Mary said: "My soul glorifies the Lord and my spirit rejoices in God my Savior, for he has been mindful of the humble state of his servant. From now on all generations will call me blessed, for the Mighty One has done great things for me—holy is his name."
LUKE 1:46–49 NIV

When we think of Mary, we think of God's perfect choice to bring human Jesus into this world, of the best mother to raise a young Savior. And we're right, but Mary's own words tell us she saw her role in a different light. She lived to serve her God, and in that way, we can all be just like her.

We can remember Mary's choice when our own work seems hard, and we can look at all we do as a beautiful chance to serve in the way God's chosen. None of us has Mary's responsibility, but each member of your family has a life equally set aside by God to serve His purposes. We can trust that God's given us each a game plan as surely as we can trust He selected Mary. And we can meet Him right there in the manger, just as she did.

Every choice we make to serve today leads us to more opportunity tomorrow. It's a gift He's given us—to be able to partner with Him and make a difference in the lives of those around us. In your home, caring for each other and loving and helping each other serves God.

In your community, telling others about our Savior and sharing what you have with them serves God. Every act small or large that shows God to someone else is an act of worship. It's God's gift we have the pleasure of giving away again and again, Christmas Day and every day.

Prayer

Father, thank You for giving us so many opportunities to worship You by serving You. Please show us how to serve You today.

Activity

Choose a service you can do as a family, perhaps invite a new neighbor for a meal or help a relative with shopping or cleaning. Talk to your children as you work about Jesus and how we're worshipping Him and serving Him when we reach out to others in help or support, and that's a gift to Him from us!

Good King Wenceslas

Sire, the night is darker now,
and the wind blows stronger,
Fails my heart, I know not how;
I can go no longer.
Mark my footsteps, my good page,
tread thou in them boldly,
Thou shalt find the winter's rage
freeze thy blood less coldly.

In his master's steps he trod
where the snow lay dinted
Heat was in the very sod which
the saint had printed
Therefore Christian men be sure,
wealth or rank possessing,
Ye who now will bless the poor,
shall yourselves find blessing.

December 6
Prepared and Ready

In those days Caesar Augustus issued a decree that a census should be taken of the entire Roman world. (This was the first census that took place while Quirinius was governor of Syria.) And everyone went to their own town to register.
LUKE 2:1–3 NIV

Hundreds of years before Christ's human birth, God prepared the world for Him and prepared the way for His earthly parents to arrive in the little town of Bethlehem. Today God continues to prepare for us, because He's in everything we do. Sometimes we see, and sometimes we don't.

Even when we don't understand a situation or see how something routine or unremarkable could be God's work, we can pay attention and open ourselves up to His guidance by taking nothing for granted, by serving with a willing heart.

Time spent with family and friends is preparation for something wonderful. Kindness to strangers and patience in difficulty is preparation for something wonderful. Private, quiet time listening to God and learning about Him is preparation for something wonderful. Christmas reminds us of His attention to detail and long-range planning, and He's granted us the gift of being part of His work that still goes on today.

We all have many "Bethlehems" we're headed to in our lives, and God will see that we're prepared when we get there. He will prepare the way and prepare us for the way. Jesus' carefully planned birth reminds us of that, and His life enables us to be part of all that's to come.

Prayer

Father, thank You for the gift of Your divine preparation and please help us prepare for all You've planned for our family today and always.

Activity

At the census in Bethlehem, Mary and Joseph and the other people were counted. Help your children count something else— days. On your family calendar or a big, colorful calendar just for the kids, on each day starting today, draw a heart or a cross and tell your children that that symbol will remind all of you to pray every day to be prepared for God's will. Pray as a family and encourage your children to say their private prayers, too.

O Little Town of Bethlehem

O little town of Bethlehem,
how still we see thee lie!
Above thy deep and dreamless sleep
the silent stars go by.
Yet in thy dark streets shineth
the everlasting Light;
The hopes and fears of all the years
are met in thee tonight.

For Christ is born of Mary
And gathered all above
While mortals sleep, the angels keep
Their watch of wondering love
O morning stars together
Proclaim the holy birth
And praises sing to God the King
And Peace to men on earth.

DECEMBER 7
Home and Home Again

So Joseph also went up from the town of Nazareth
in Galilee to Judea, to Bethlehem the town of David,
because he belonged to the house and line of David.
He went there to register with Mary, who was pledged
to be married to him and was expecting a child.
LUKE 2:4–5 NIV

The journey Joseph and Mary would take to the delivery room God had chosen was a journey back to their homeland, back to where their story began and a long-passed-on prophet knew: "Out of [Bethlehem] will come for me one who will be ruler over Israel, whose origins are from of old, from ancient times" (Micah 5:2 NIV).

"Home" is where we meet God, where we have Christmas every day, where we rest knowing God is in charge and we don't have to be. Coming home to our families each night brings us joy and peace, and working through our days to get home to God every second allows so much more. We meet God in the blessings He showers on us, in the friends who help and support us, in the family members who love us and journey with us. And we keep going, because no matter how scared we might get at some intersections or unknown roads, we know God is waiting, holding arms open wide to welcome us in, so glad to be with us even if we get a little lost or sidetracked along the way.

God knows our steps, and when we trust them to Him, we, like Mary and Joseph, will find safe passage and the delivery room for all we've been created to bring forth, too. We can trust Jesus to be there, as home and home again we go.

Prayer

Father, thank You for always planning the perfect journey for us. Help us trust You and follow You unafraid.

Activity

Have mom or dad promise each child they'll be somewhere with a big hug when the child finds them. Then have one parent or an older child walk each child a long and winding route through the house or yard to get to the other parent. When the child arrives, have the parent keep his or her promise.

Joseph Dearest

"Joseph dearest, Joseph mine,
Help me cradle the Child divine;
God reward thee and all that's thine
In paradise," so prays the mother Mary.

He came among us at Christmas time
At Christmas time in Bethlehem
Men shall bring him from far and wide,
Love's diadem: Jesus, Jesus;
Lo, he comes and loves and saves and frees us.

"Gladly, dear one, lady mine,
Help I cradle this child of thine;
God's own light on us both shall shine
In paradise, as prays the mother Mary."

December 8
Chosen Today

"I am the LORD your God, who teaches you what is best for you, who directs you in the way you should go."
ISAIAH 48:17 NIV

Mary's donkey was sure-footed and stable, just the right creature for the job of transporting our Savior and His mother. God chose the destination and the route—and He also chose the method to accomplish this most important goal, and He's still doing that in our lives today.

God chooses the family to give us and the abilities and talents and gifts to give each one of us. At Christmas, we may tend to focus on the tangible gifts we give others and the gifts of love and grace God has given us in Jesus. We also want to remember all the other gifts He's given us so that we can play our parts in His continually unfolding story starring Jesus.

God has many jobs to get done, and getting Mary safely to Bethlehem was one of them, so He chose the right donkey from among all the other donkeys in the world. Today, He chooses you and your family members from all the other people in the world to do the jobs only you can do. He knows what we're all best at, and He gives us the opportunity to experience that great joy of working with Him to accomplish His goals.

God trusts us completely with the jobs He's set aside for us. As we keep His destination and route in mind, we learn how to be the vehicle to help others, show them who God is, introduce them to Jesus, and be their friend along the way.

Prayer

Father, thank You for giving us jobs as important as You gave the donkey carrying Mary and Jesus, and please help us do what we do best for You.

Activity

Give each child a simple destination (another room), a simple route (around the corner), and ask him or her to be the method to deliver something there: Have a child carry a love note or tiny gift to another family member in the other room. Explain that's how God works with us—giving us a job to share Him with others however we can.

The Friendly Beasts

Jesus, our brother, strong and good,
was humbly born in a stable rude,
and the friendly beasts around him stood,
Jesus, our brother, strong and good.

"I," said the donkey, shaggy and brown,
"I carried his mother uphill and down,
I carried his mother to Bethlehem town;
I," said the donkey, shaggy and brown.

"I," said the sheep with curly horn,
"I gave him my wool for his blanket warm;
he wore my coat on Christmas morn;
I," said the sheep with curly horn.

Thus all the beasts, by some good spell,
in the stable dark were glad to tell
of the gifts they gave Emmanuel,
the gifts they gave Emmanuel.

December 9
Promises Now and Forever

*"Your house and your kingdom shall endure before Me
forever; your throne shall be established forever."*
2 SAMUEL 7:16 NASB

Today, we remember God's promises of old that apply to us. Christmas reminds us of the best promise ever made and kept. And Jesus learned well from His Father. His word to be with us always (Matthew 28:20) and His words of peace (John 14:27) and rest (Matthew 11:28) and victory (John 16:33) comfort us when times are hard and embolden us when work awaits. And perhaps Jesus modeled those promises for us so that we could follow.

No matter what, no matter when, no matter where—you can faithfully promise your family members to be with them in their hearts, to support them up close or far away, to remain loyal and trusting forevermore. You can promise to be a sanctuary, a safe place, a comfort zone they can always find. You can make these promises because God and Jesus make and keep Their promises and will help you keep yours. It's a gift of follow-through we experience the more we lean on Their promises and claim those promises for ourselves.

Children will come to learn that some promises, like God's promise of Jesus, take a long time to come to pass, but that doesn't make them any less true. Our promises are only to be made with great thought and sincere intentions, so let God's track record guide us at Christmas and always.

Prayer

Father, thank You for Your promises that always come to life, and for Christmas when we celebrate the greatest promise of all.

Activity

Have each family member write or draw a picture of a promise to another family member—for example, a young child can promise a hug for mom or dad. Put each promise in an envelope or small box and place it under your Christmas tree. Open the promises Christmas Eve and have each family member follow through.

O Come, O Come, Emmanuel

O come, O come, Emmanuel,
And ransom captive Israel,
That mourns in lonely exile here
Until the Son of God appear.

Rejoice! Rejoice! Emmanuel
Shall come to thee, O Israel.

O come, Thou Day-spring, come and cheer
Our spirits by Thine advent here;
Disperse the gloomy clouds of night,
And death's dark shadows put to flight.

Rejoice! Rejoice! Emmanuel
Shall come to thee, O Israel.

O come, Thou Key of David, come,
And open wide our heavenly home;
Make safe the way that leads on high,
And close the path to misery.

Rejoice! Rejoice! Emmanuel
Shall come to thee, O Israel.

Knowing What's Important

And she brought forth her firstborn Son, and wrapped
Him in swaddling cloths, and laid Him in a manger,
because there was no room for them in the inn.
LUKE 2:7 NKJV

We would imagine that, after a long journey and when about to deliver the world's Savior, Mary and Joseph were exhausted yet excited, eager to get to a comfortable resting place. Perhaps they were scared when there was no place to stay and no bed for Mary and the Baby. Perhaps they were confused, wondering why God wouldn't provide for them what they needed to serve in this very special way. Or perhaps they trusted that He was providing. Perhaps they trusted that He had not forgotten about their most important mission. Perhaps they trusted each step that led them to the manger.

Christmas reminds us to trust God's sovereign plan even if we get scared or confused. Christmas reminds us that God's methods may seem unusual sometimes, and we may not understand every turn or development, but He is always in control. He showed us His perfect attention to detail and planning when He chose the place for His most important gift. And He left everything less important somewhere else. That's a guide we can use—the best choice is always to follow God and let everything else less important settle somewhere else. Christmas is a beautiful celebration of Mary and Joseph's trust, and that's a gift they still give to us today.

Prayer

Father, thank You for always having the perfect plan for Your will and for helping us know what we need to know to do our most important work.

Activity

Get an empty first-aid kit and let your children put silly things in the box—toys, spoons, crayons, anything that would be useless for first aid. Help them see that something full of the less important stuff isn't what we need, and the inn was full of everything less important than Jesus, so Mary and Joseph didn't need it –they only needed to trust and follow God.

Away with Our Fears!

Away with our fears!
The Godhead appears
In Christ reconciled
The Father of mercies in Jesus the Child.

He comes from above,
In manifest love,
Desire of our eyes,
The meek Lamb of God, in a manger He lies.

Immanuel's birth
What triumph on earth!
Yet could it afford
No better a place for its heavenly Lord?

The Ancient of Days
Redeems a lost race:
His glory comes down
Self-humbled to carry us up to a crown.

A Manger Spoken For

So it was, that while they were there, the days were completed for her to be delivered. And she brought forth her firstborn Son, and wrapped Him in swaddling cloths, and laid Him in a manger, because there was no room for them in the inn.
LUKE 2:6–7 NKJV

We might read that part of the Christmas story and wonder how that no-vacancy detail could have escaped God's attention. How could He have failed to make room at the inn for His Son and His family? But look again, and we'll see something else.

That manger wasn't an afterthought or backup plan if something else didn't work out. It was a gift, a tangible demonstration of God's focus and order, because there was room for only one Savior. And the gift from old is re-created each day in our hearts where, again, there is room for only one Savior.

Is your heart running low on peace or joy, trust or belief or eagerness to live your life? Whatever your heart needs is wrapped perfectly in the gift of the living Christ—joy to the world at His birth and right now, too.

And as surely as He filled that manger designed only for Him, He fills your heart with the grace and will and power you need to live the life He's designed only for you, because you are no afterthought or backup plan either.

Because He is our greatest teacher and example, we learn to live this beautiful life as we make room in the manger of our hearts for the peace and joy He's created especially for us. And Christmas is a wonderful time to begin.

Prayer

Father, thank You for the manger You planned and our Jesus to fill it and for our family and our Jesus to fill our hearts.

Activity

Look at as many pictures as you can find of nativity scenes: in books, on the computer, on greeting cards. Gather any nativity scenes you have, perhaps even unveil a new one for your family, or draw or make a simple one together. Ask your children how many Saviors are in each nativity. The answer is always one—the One God sent because there could be no other. Remind your children how special and unique Jesus is and how our hearts are designed to hold only Him.

Joy to the World

Joy to the world, the Lord is come!
Let earth receive her King;
Let every heart prepare Him room,
And heaven and nature sing,
And heaven and nature sing,
And Heaven, and heaven, and nature sing.
Joy to the earth, the Savior reigns!
Let men their songs employ;
While fields and floods, rocks, hills and plains
Repeat the sounding joy,
Repeat the sounding joy,
Repeat, repeat, the sounding joy.

No more let sins and sorrows grow,
Nor thorns infest the ground;
He comes to make His blessings flow
Far as the curse is found,
Far as the curse is found,
Far as, far as, the curse is found.
He rules the world with truth and grace,
And makes the nations prove
The glories of His righteousness,
And wonders of His love,
And wonders of His love,
And wonders, wonders, of His love.

*And she brought forth her firstborn Son, and wrapped
Him in swaddling cloths, and laid Him in a manger,
because there was no room for them in the inn.*
LUKE 2:7 NKJV

When Jesus Son of man (John 3:13) was baby Jesus in the manger, He was truly one of us, needing a loving mother's tender care—and Mary met His needs, wrapping Him in cloths warm and soft, holding Him close, cradling the head He couldn't yet hold up, measuring her breath to His. In the very beginning, life for our Savior was simple.

And Jesus Son of God (John 11:27) has been meeting our needs ever since, at the beginning, middle, or end of anything. He wraps us in His love, cradles our fearful and hurting hearts, and measures out the grace we need to carry on. It's a gift of focus on us as if we're all He has to tend to, the only needy baby in the house.

We can trust Him to respond to our every cry the way Mary responded to Jesus' baby whimpers, His childhood hurts—the human side of His world. He knows well how important to us fragile and insecure sheep a close and powerful Shepherd is. He knows and He responds, with guidance and peace, the Son of God close as man needs, Christmas alive every moment.

Prayer

Father, thank You for Jesus' human birth and life and His wonderful ability to know just what we need.

Activity

Gather some strips of cloth, towels, or old clothing. Hold your children close and gently wrap the cloths around them and say with each wrap something like, "Jesus brings His love, Jesus brings His peace, Jesus is listening to you." And tell them that His focus on them is just as secure as your arms around them right now.

Away in a Manger

Away in a manger, no crib for a bed,
The little Lord Jesus laid down his sweet head.
The stars in the bright sky looked down where he lay,
The little Lord Jesus asleep on the hay.

The cattle are lowing, the poor Baby wakes,
But little Lord Jesus, no crying He makes.
I love Thee, Lord Jesus; look down from the sky
And stay by my cradle till morning is nigh.

Be near me, Lord Jesus; I ask Thee to stay
Close by me forever and love me I pray!
Bless all the dear children in Thy tender care,
And fit us for heaven to live with Thee there.

DECEMBER 13
Shepherding Us Now

And there were shepherds living out in the fields nearby,
keeping watch over their flocks at night.
LUKE 2:8 NIV

The shepherds in the fields seem unlikely representatives of our Lord; but it's no mistake, because we are so much like the wayward sheep they tended. And knowing our every need, God sent us a Shepherd. Just like the caring and watchful shepherd knows every sheep, Jesus knows each of us inside and out, our needs and weaknesses, so He, too, keeps watch over His flock, day and night.

The sheep in the field can't get where they're going on their own. They don't know where the best grazing fields are, where the fresh streams of water are, how to fight off predators or battle the elements. But their shepherd does. And he stays with them, nearby, guiding and protecting. That's why the comparison between the shepherd of the field and the Shepherd of our lives is right as a star atop your tree.

We, too, can't get by on our own; and because of Jesus, we don't have to. He will stay with us, nearby, guiding and protecting us. He will show us where our life's work is and then walk with us every step. And if we'll continue to be like the shepherd's sheep and trust the shepherd—our Shepherd—we'll know the unending celebration of Christmas as we journey through all the fields of our lives.

Prayer

Father, thank You for Jesus' understanding of our sheeplike ways and for being the Shepherd we need every day.

Activity

Have each child make or draw a candy cane or use a real (wrapped) one. Tell your children that the cane represents Jesus the Shepherd who always watches over us. Place each candy cane near each child's bed or affix it to the door as a reminder that Jesus is closer than a thought and can always be trusted to guide and protect us.

The First Noel

The first Noel the angel did say
Was to certain poor shepherds in fields as they lay;
In fields where they lay keeping their sheep,
On a cold winter's night that was so deep.
Noel, Noel, Noel, Noel,
Born is the King of Israel.

They looked up and saw a star
Shining in the east beyond them far:
And to the earth it gave great light
And so it continued both day and night.
Noel, Noel, Noel, Noel,
Born is the King of Israel.

December 14
Unafraid

*And behold, an angel of the Lord stood
before them, and the glory of the Lord shone
around them, and they were greatly afraid.*
LUKE 2:9 NKJV

When Jesus was born, the "glory of the Lord" around the shepherds was all they could see, and they were frightened and confused. Sometimes our fears become all we can see, but God is bigger.

Whenever we're scared, we need to remember that God is there, no matter what we see. His glory is on us, waiting to shine through us for others to see.

We always have the possibility of discovering and creating great things from whatever happens— because Jesus is steadying us in our fears so that we can see what to do next. No matter what the experience, the place to look for help is always in our hearts where Jesus lives.

We can think of our fear as one big bubble around us and then picture it full of Jesus. He smiles at us and holds us close so that all the fear seeps out like air from a tiny hole in a tricycle tire. Then when we're calm and secure in His presence, we're able to see the possibility of everything remaining—the possibility of learning more about His love and our purpose here, of being more a part of how He touches those around us. It's a possibility we don't want to miss out of fear, and Jesus says we never have to.

Prayer

Lord, thank You for removing our fears
as Jesus pushes them away and helps us see
what He'll do next in our lives.

Activity

Turn off all the lights so that your family members are unable to see each other
(take care younger ones aren't upset).
Then light a candle and see how quickly
everyone's faces come into view, hidden by
the darkness but there all along. Explain to
your children that Jesus fills up the scared
spaces in us just like the candlelight fills up
the darkness, and because of Him so near,
great joys await.

While Shepherds Watched Their Flocks

While shepherds watched their flocks by night,
All seated on the ground,
The angel of the Lord came down,
And glory shone around,
And glory shone around.
"Fear not!" said he, for mighty dread
Had seized their troubled mind.
"Glad tidings of great joy I bring
To you and all mankind
To you and all mankind.'"

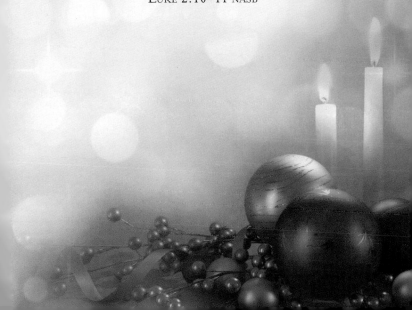

DECEMBER 15
Just for You

But the angel said to them, "Do not be afraid; for behold,
I bring you good news of great joy which will be for all the
people; for today in the city of David there has been born
for you a Savior, who is Christ the Lord."
LUKE 2:10–11 NASB

The angel reassured the shepherds that their Savior had come, for them, for each of them and just as sure, He came for us, for each of us. The Christ Child King already knew each of those shepherds' hearts and souls and how they would go on to bring glory to Him—and He was prepared to give them what they needed.

Since that Christmas morning, His knowing and giving continues. For every one of us who waits in the pastures or classrooms or workplaces of our lives and needs our Savior close, He came.

He came with big plans, too, plans for us and our families because we are all special, unique, and deeply loved children of God. The shepherds received a personal announcement of His arrival, and each Christmas morning is ours.

Like a beautifully wrapped present for each of us as big as the whole world, He holds great wonders yet unseen; and because of Him and His grace, we can become what He already sees: disciples like the shepherds with important work to do. And Jesus joys in that, in each one of us able to do our specific job for Him, that He's already chosen. It's a gift of His intimacy for each of us.

Prayer

Father, thank You for sending Jesus for each of us, and for helping us become what He already sees.

Activity

Make a simple birth announcement for Jesus out of construction paper, one for each family member. On the inside, note Jesus' name, place of birth, and the reason (God loves me). On the outside of each announcement, write a family member's name because Jesus came for each one of us. Remind your children how special they all are and how Jesus will use their lives to do amazing things only they can do.

It Came Upon the Midnight Clear

It came upon the midnight clear,
That glorious song of old,
From angels bending near the earth,
To touch their harps of gold;
"Peace on the earth, good will to men,
From Heaven's all gracious King!"
The world in solemn stillness lay,
To hear the angels sing.

Still through the cloven skies they come
With peaceful wings unfurled,
And still their heavenly music floats
O'er all the weary world;
Above its sad and lowly plains,
They bend on hovering wing,
And ever over its Babel sounds
The blessèd angels sing.

DECEMBER 16
Signs Everywhere

*"And this will be the sign to you: You will find a
Babe wrapped in swaddling cloths, lying in a manger."*
LUKE 2:12 NKJV

The sweet, tiny Babe who made His human entry into our world was long awaited and gladly welcomed. He was a breathing, growing, smiling sign of God's love for all who would receive Him.

But God wasn't done. He sends us other signs today, signs to guide, equip, inspire, and support us and our families in everything we do.

We have a sign of God's grace in the loving people who forgive us and help us when we fail. We have a sign of His faith in us in the second, third, or seventy-third chance He gives us to follow His will. We have a sign of His delight in us in the joys we experience in our lives including our family time at Christmas and beyond.

When we pay attention to God's signs, we'll be as amazed as the shepherds, blown away but steadied to the core by His limitless generosity and unfailing ability to speak to us and give to us what we need. Let's keep looking.

And let's also take note of the opportunities to be a sign of God's love to those around us, at home, school, work, and play. Encouragement, support, forgiveness, courage, understanding—every good and God-inspired gift we give is a sign of Him to those who need Him. Let's keep looking.

Christmas, past or beyond, the signs just keep coming. Gifts abound.

Prayer

Father, thank You for Your signs and the chance to be one, and please help us not to miss any.

Activity

Create a private "sign" for your family that means "I love you," something such as a tug on the ear, fingers crossed, or something the children choose. Help your children make the sign to their other parent, and begin and end each day with it, reminding them of God's signs of love everywhere. Keep looking!

While Shepherds Watched Their Flocks

"To you, in David's town, this day
Is born of David's line
A Savior, who is Christ the Lord,
And this shall be the sign,
And this shall be the sign.

"The heavenly Babe you there shall find
To human view displayed,
All meanly wrapped in swathing bands,
And in a manger laid,
And in a manger laid."
"All glory be to God on high,
And to the Earth be peace;
Good will henceforth from Heav'n to men
Begin and never cease,
Begin and never cease!"

Cattle Lowing, Us Loving

You will go out in joy and be led forth in peace;
the mountains and hills will burst into song before you,
and all the trees of the field will clap their hands.
Isaiah 55:12 NIV

God made each of us unique, one-of-a-kind, in this big, full world. He knows each one of us by every little thing we do and every thought and dream we have. God's gift of individuality, of one-of-a-kind-ness allows each of us to worship and serve in the way we know best.

Babies are often comforted by the low, steady sounds of animals, and those surrounding baby Jesus did their part to celebrate His physical entry into our world. "The cattle are lowing, the baby awakes, But little Lord Jesus, no crying he makes. . . ." Not able to speak of course, but able to honor Him just the same, the animals did what they could with what they had, each one doing his best. That's all God asks of us.

Each decision we make to praise God and tell Jesus's story in the way only we can is the perfect use of our gift of individuality, our one-of-a-kindness. God only asks that we love our Savior nonstop and never feel our efforts are less than anyone else's. Everything we do to honor Jesus, when it comes from our heart and is the best we can offer, says, "I love You" to Him, and that's always right.

Christmas is a time to remember that Jesus is One, but He's able to speak to each of us—and hear each of us—in the best way for each of us. May our celebrations today be a comfort to Him as the animals in the stable were that beautiful morning.

Prayer

Father, thank You for understanding our words and thoughts and actions as we celebrate Jesus in our own way.

Activity

Look at a family portrait or snapshot, and appreciate the differences among members. Allow family members to say how they would have uniquely welcomed Jesus if they'd been there with the animals. Maybe younger children will imitate the animals or draw a picture—no way is wrong as we remember that Jesus loves us each for who we are.

Carol

Goodman Joseph toiled through the snow—
Saw the star o'er a stable low;
Mary she might not further go—
Welcome thatch, and litter below!
Joy was hers in the morning!
And then they heard the angels tell
"Who were the first to cry Nowell?
Animals all, as it befell,
In the stable where they did dwell!
Joy shall be theirs in the morning!"

DECEMBER 18
Glory, Peace, and Me

And suddenly there was with the angel a multitude of the heavenly host praising God and saying: "Glory to God in the highest, and on earth peace, goodwill toward men!"
LUKE 2:13–14 NKJV

$\mathcal{G}$lory and peace always go together. It's a gift that gives us even more than we first see. The gift of praising God—giving Him the glory for all we are and all we do because He makes it all possible—takes our minds off ourselves and onto God who's in charge, and that gives us peace no matter what. Christmas helps us see that connection as we celebrate Jesus' birth and all that means. Because He has come and saved us, every day and every situation is a point of praise, and peace follows.

So when we find ourselves in pain or fear, confusion or despair, we know how to get out. We turn to God, praise Him, trust Him, and rely on Him because we know we don't have to do anything by ourselves, and we breathe in peace only He can give.

And we can help our family members when they're hurting, too. We can pray with them and help them focus on the greatness and power of God. We can remember Jesus' coming into our world so that our world would never be the same. We can give thanks to God for His close and constant care and rest in His love and grace with them. We can be a bearer of peace and help them find their own.

Glory and peace always go together. The gift we give gives back even more.

Prayer

Lord, thank You for Your gift of peace
lived out in Jesus and for helping us always
experience Your peace and glorify You at
the same time.

Activity

As a family make up a song, something
short such as "Jesus is my Lord/Jesus loves
me/So no matter what/I am at peace."
Sing the song with your children on the
way to school or daycare or when they're
getting dressed each morning. Sing it to
yourself, too!

O Come, Let Us Adore Him

O come, let us adore him,
O come let us adore him,
O come, let us adore him,
Christ the Lord.
For You alone are worthy,
For You alone are worthy,
For You alone are worthy,
Christ the Lord!

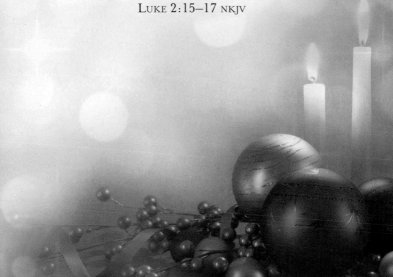

DECEMBER 19
Choosing to Share

So it was, when the angels had gone away from them into heaven, that the shepherds said to one another, "Let us now go to Bethlehem and see this thing that has come to pass, which the Lord has made known to us." And they came with haste and found Mary and Joseph, and the Babe lying in a manger. Now when they had seen Him, they made widely known the saying which was told them concerning this Child.
LUKE 2:15–17 NKJV

$\mathcal{W}$e aren't told the angels ordered the shepherds to do anything, but they decided together "let us now go. . ."; and in their excitement, they took God's gift of choice and saw their joy ripple far and wide.

We have the same gift of choice today and so very much to share. We can make "widely known" what Jesus has brought to our hearts, first among our families, and then as we reach way, way out, as wide as the sky, as deep as a hug, as pure as understanding, to all those we meet.

God doesn't give us an order or make Christmas come only if we contact ten people and tell them the story. Instead, He chooses to trust us with His gift of choice, to give us all we need to know about Jesus to share Him with someone else—that He is our Savior and He loves us all.

That we get to live that great news every day is a blessing God willingly pours on us—telling others about it is a choice we make to be a blessing to them. God's plan lets us be a part.

Prayer

Father, thank You for trusting us with the gift of choice, for allowing us to be part of Jesus' story by telling others about Him.

Activity

Have each family member choose something they like (candy, favorite toy, cherished book) and tell other family members about it, because we bring joy to others when we share what we know. Have one parent pretend not to know Jesus and have the other parent or an older child explain Christmas.

God Rest You Merry, Gentlemen

"Fear not, then," said the angel,
"Let nothing you affright,
This day is born a Savior of a pure Virgin bright,
To free all those who trust in Him
from Satan's power and might."

Now to the Lord sing praises,
All you within this place,
And with true love and brotherhood
Each other now embrace;
This holy tide of Christmas
Doth bring redeeming grace.

DECEMBER 20
Time Well Spent

And all who heard it were amazed at what th
shepherds said to them. But Mary treasured
up all these things and pondered them in her heart.
LUKE 2:18–19 NIV

Jesus must have been the talk of the fields and streets as more and more people heard about His arrival. How did Joseph and Mary handle those who wanted to worship their Babe?

We know Mary wanted time alone with her Father. And because we so often need the same thing, God grants us His gift of solitude—time alone with Him because He wants time alone with each of us.

The gift of solitude and special time with God as if you're the only person in the world blesses you and pleases Him. Yes, the Christmas season brings activities and parties and fun times with family and friends, but let's not neglect this special gift because it's one of God's favorites, when He gets to spend uninterrupted time with us, talking, listening, quiet.

Jesus was human and understood this need and frequently left His disciples and went away to pray to His Father alone, and He was always strengthened afterward. When we claim God's gift of solitude with Him and take time away to pray, we're strengthened, too, renewed and reignited. Taking time to "ponder"—to talk and listen to God—will help us learn from the past and plan for the future. God still makes time for all His children, so let's all make time for Him, at Christmas and always.

Prayer

Father, thank You for the private world we share with You, for Jesus who made it possible at Christmas and always.

Activity

Make each family member a little four-page storybook to look at in private time with God—just pieces of construction paper, canvas, or even cut up paper plates stapled together. Pages can be simple drawings, favorite Bible verses, pictures cut from magazines or newspapers, blank pages for adults, or prayers written for little ones.

O Little Town of Bethlehem

How silently, how silently,
the wondrous Gift is giv'n;
So God imparts to human
hearts the blessings of His Heav'n.
No ear may hear His coming,
but in this world of sin,
Where meek souls will receive Him,
still, the dear Christ enters in.

Where children pure and happy
pray to the blessèd Child,
Where misery cries out to Thee,
Son of the mother mild;
Where charity stands watching
and faith holds wide the door,
The dark night wakes, the glory breaks,
and Christmas comes once more.

DECEMBER 21
"This Way"

Now after Jesus was born in Bethlehem of Judea in the days of Herod the king, behold, wise men from the East came to Jerusalem, saying, "Where is He who has been born King of the Jews? For we have seen His star in the East and have come to worship Him."
MATTHEW 2:1–2 NKJV

When Jesus first came into our world, those who heard of His arrival had the privilege of directing others to Him. And even though He's not arriving again as a Holy Babe, people today still need help in getting to Him. And that's where we get to play a part—we have the same privilege today: the gift of directing others to Jesus.

Sometimes we'll encounter people who seem afraid to trust Jesus, but we can help them see that Jesus takes away our fears because He's bigger and more powerful than anything that could frighten us.

Sometimes we'll encounter people who seem unsure that Jesus can love them because they haven't always loved Him, but we can help them see that Jesus always loves us first and will never turn us away if we make the choice to follow Him. Sometimes we'll encounter people who seem confused about Jesus and need to hear our story, and we can help them by telling them how everything began at Christmas and will never end because Jesus is our Savior who will never abandon us. We can direct them to Him by guiding them with our own lives, by being both an example and a road map that those who don't know Jesus can use to get to Him.

It's a beautiful gift God's given us—let's not miss an opportunity to be wise and generous with our directions.

Prayer

Father, thank You for those around us who need directions to Jesus and for the opportunity to help guide them.

Activity

Draw a simple, colorful map with your children, including "You are here" marked with a star, a path labeled "Jesus' Way," and then the destination labeled "Peace and Love"—because that's what traveling with Jesus gives us. Let each family member take the path on the map with a game piece or other small item. Remind your children that they're never too young to give "Jesus directions."

We Three Kings

We three kings of Orient are;
Bearing gifts we traverse afar,
Field and fountain, moor and mountain,
Following yonder star.

O, star of wonder, star of light,
Star with royal beauty bright,
Westward leading, still proceeding,
Guide us to thy perfect light.

Born a king on Bethlehem's plain
Gold I bring to crown Him again,
King forever, ceasing never,
Over us all to reign.

O star of wonder, star of light,
Star with royal beauty bright,
Westward leading, still proceeding,
Guide us to thy perfect light.

DECEMBER 22
Free in Surrender

When Herod the king heard this, he was troubled,
and all Jerusalem with him. . . . Then Herod, when he
had secretly called the wise men, determined from them
what time the star appeared. And he sent them to Bethlehem
and said, "Go and search carefully for the young Child,
and when you have found Him, bring back word to me,
that I may come and worship Him also."
MATTHEW 2:3, 7–8 NKJV

King Herod was afraid, "troubled," and threatened by what he didn't understand. Because he was afraid of having to give up his power to a superior king, he turned to a life of trickery, deceit, and suspicion, when he could've chosen to worship the Christ Child instead.

Sadly, he misunderstood Jesus' power, believing that it was power that took away from him when it's actually power that gives to us more than we can imagine.

No earthly king can set us free when we surrender to him, but that's exactly what Jesus does. The best order for our lives is Jesus at the top, our Savior who came on Christmas to be with us forever. Surrendering to Him means simply opening our hearts so that we have Him to guide and direct us in every situation we face. And in surrendering to Him, we are free, in bondage to no one, to no ideals that are counter to our Lord's.

Families together are strong and protective, and we willingly surrender to the circle of those we love. Our surrendering to Jesus makes us strong and protected, and it's a choice we get to make and encourage others to make, too. Christmas is a great time for surrender.

Prayer

Father, thank You for the kingdom of our hearts where Jesus rules and for the choice to surrender to You and live in peace.

Activity

Draw a basic organizational chart with a box for Jesus at the top, an arrow drawn down, and a photo or simple drawing of each family member. Explain to your children that when Jesus is in charge of our lives, we're free of worry and fear because we trust God to be in control and hold us safely in His hands.

The First Noel

They looked up and saw a star
Shining in the east, beyond them far;
And to the earth it gave great light,
And so it continued both day and night.

And by the light of that same star,
Three wise men came from country far;
To seek for a King was their intent,
And to follow the star wherever it went.
Noel, Noel, Noel, Noel,
Born is the King of Israel.

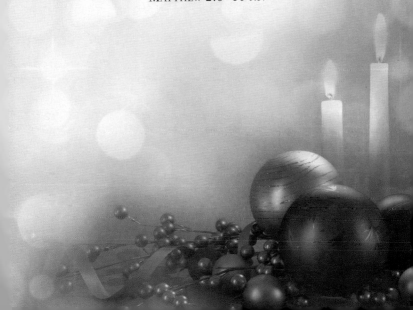

DECEMBER 23
Overjoyed

After they had heard the king, they went on their way,
and the star they had seen when it rose went ahead of
them until it stopped over the place where the child was.
When they saw the star, they were overjoyed.
MATTHEW 2:9–10 NIV

$\mathcal{P}$erhaps Baby Jesus wasn't surprised by the "overjoyed" reaction of the wise men, because He has been doing everything for us "overwell" ever since. He overloves us, overguides us and overprotects us—and the gift we've been given of Jesus' overattention causes us to be overjoyed, too.

That's because we learn His habits and His tendency to be overpresent in our lives—present when we call His name and present when we don't even think about it. He's present because He loves us more than we know and looks out for us more closely than we can understand.

He's overinterested in everything on our minds, so no matter how small something may seem in relation to great concerns, Jesus cares and keeps His attention focused on our every thought, hurt, fear, and feeling. He understands everything we can't and sees all our situations and problems from every angle. He stands ready to help in every way we'll allow. He just can't do anything in a small way.

Christmas reminds us of the journey of the wise men to see Jesus—let it remind us of His journey to be with us, each one of us, with the overattention only He can provide.

Prayer

Father, thank You for receiving our love and loving us back through Jesus more than we can understand.

Activity

Look at a book in the dark with a pen-light—that represents often as much as we can see. Then look at the book with a spot-light or the brightest flashlight you have—that's how Jesus sees everything going on in our lives. He provides overcare for us, a gift of greater love, more than we can "see" and never less than we need.

The First Noel

Then did they know assuredly
Within that house the King did lie:
One entered in then for to see,
And found the Babe in poverty:
Noel, Noel, Noel, Noel!
Born is the King of Israel!

Then entered in those wise men three
Full reverently upon their knee,
And offered there in His presence
Their gold, and myrrh and frankincense.
Noel, Noel, Noel, Noel!
Born is the King of Israel!

On coming to the house, they saw the child with his mother Mary, and they bowed down and worshiped him. Then they opened their treasures and presented him with gifts of gold, frankincense and myrrh.
MATTHEW 2:11 NIV

*T*hose men traveled full-handed to present gifts of the best their culture knew to the best gift our world would ever know. A couple thousand years later and we're still traveling to Him, bearing gifts of the best we have, and we learn that it's us—our love and devotion and faith and trust and service. Our life is the most cherished gift our Savior receives, because that's how we can be part of helping others know Him.

And the wise men showed us how—they worshipped the Lord Jesus first and then presented their gifts. They understood the first Noel and set for us and our families an example of God's wishes at Christmas and beyond: worship our Savior because He's our Savior and then honor the King with all we have to give. This order brings Christmas alive year-round because we come to see that worship is in everything we do, and giving our best is a gift that we live.

It's a never-ending Christmas celebration to represent Jesus to those around us. So when we love Him by loving others in every little or big way we know, every day of the year, He sees a birthday gift, and the joy continues.

Prayer

Father, thank You for the opportunity to give all we are to You, on Christmas and always, to worship You by giving to others.

Activity

Draw a simple picture of each family member or print a small copy from your computer. Let each person sign his photo "love, name" and roll it up like a piece of taffy. Secure the ends with Christmas ribbon and add a gift tag: "To: God. From: me." Place each rolled photo under the Christmas tree and explain to your children that the best and most lasting gift we can give God is the gift of ourselves to live for Him. When we give ourselves to Him, we allow the best life He's planned for us to come to light, starting at Christmas.

The Wise Men Bring Their Learning

The wise may bring their learning,
the rich may bring their wealth,
And some may bring their greatness,
and some bring strength and health;
We, too, would bring our
treasures to offer to the King;
We have no wealth or learning;
what shall we children bring?
We'll bring Him hearts that love Him;
we'll bring Him thankful praise,
And young souls meekly
striving to walk in holy ways;

And these shall be the treasures
we offer to the King,
And these are gifts that even
the poorest child may bring.
We'll bring the little duties
we have to do each day;
We'll try our best to please Him,
at home, at school, at play;
And better are these treasures
to offer to our King;
Than richest gifts without them—
yet these a child may bring.

December 25
Our Breathing Gift of Grace

For it is by grace you have been saved, through faith—
and this is not from yourselves, it is the gift of God.
EPHESIANS 2:8 NIV

Every year at Christmastime, we think of the New Year coming—and the chance to make it better than the last because of God's gift of grace. We'll grow as followers of Christ, grow within our families, have the opportunity to work toward new goals, accomplish much, and plan much more. The calendar keeps time, but God makes it all possible.

He takes our mistakes and missteps and gives us new opportunities in their place so that we can accept His grace and make better choices next time. It's His love for us lived out loud in everything we do because of Jesus' coming to life in this world with us. Without our Savior, a new day or new year or new opportunity would mean nothing. Because of Him, each moment means everything.

Jesus helps us start over and make things better whether it's the New Year or not—because we need a new beginning like the miracle of Christmas, and He says we can have it any time we humbly ask and prepare to receive. God accepts our wounded hearts and erases everything that hurts—because of the greatest Gift of our Jesus. Every year we have Christmas to remind us, and in every breath we have Him close enough to tell us.

Prayer

Father, thank You for a festive red and green reminder of Your greatest Gift every year—the greatest Gift that lasts forever.

Activity

Wrap a small empty box and hang it as an ornament or place it under your tree to represent God's grace living through Jesus. The small box's emptiness that your children can't touch or photograph is like God's grace that can't be contained because it's limitless and Jesus is everywhere. Let the box be a reminder you bring out at Christmas each year.

O Holy Night

O holy night, the stars are brightly shining;
It is the night of the dear Savior's birth!
Long lay the world in sin and error pining,
Till He appeared and the soul felt its worth.
A thrill of hope, the weary soul rejoices,
For yonder breaks a new and glorious morn.

Fall on your knees
Oh hear the angel voices
Oh night divine
Oh night when Christ was born
Oh night divine, oh night, oh night divine!

Chains shall He break
For the slave is our brother
And in His name all oppression shall cease
Sweet hymns of joy
In grateful chorus raise we
Let all within us praise His holy name

Fall on your knees
Oh hear the angel voices
Oh night divine
Oh night when Christ was born
Oh night divine, oh night, oh night divine!

Looking for more activities for your family?
Here are 31 ideas to take you all the way
through the month of December:

December 1: It is a tradition in many homes to find the annual
Christmas tree the day after Thanksgiving. Putting up the tree
can top the list as one of the greatest family activities of all time
no matter when you choose to accomplish the wonderful task.
Find a tree farm that will let you cut down your own. Many
places will take you into the woods on a wagon or in a sleigh
and serve hot chocolate or other special treats.

December 2: Make your own Advent calendar. Spend time
as a family each day counting down the days until Christmas.
One way to do this is to make a paper chain, adding one
link every morning and using it to decorate your tree on
Christmas Eve.

December 3: Contact your church and find out what
ministries or charities your church is supporting this year.
Then get involved! Many churches participate in Operation
Christmas Child, an outreach project that involves filling
shoe boxes with toys and school supplies for children in need
all over the world. Have each child in your family fill a shoe
box for a needy child. They will have fun picking out gifts
for someone else, and the project helps to keep the focus on
others. To find out more about Operation Christmas Child,
go to www.samaritanspurse.org.

December 4: Purchase mini Christmas trees and let each
child decorate his or her own. Put the trees in bedrooms,
bathrooms, or anywhere that could use an extra touch of
Christmas. Maybe even put one in the garage or barn to
brighten the day of someone working hard. Younger children
can make their own garlands from construction paper or
string popcorn or cranberries. Have some hot chocolate and
cookies on hand, and everyone will want to join in the fun!

December 5: After dinner one evening, share memories of Christmases past. Talk about favorite ornaments on the tree and where they came from. Tell about your favorite Christmas as a child or special traditions you remember. You and your children will enjoy hearing what each family member has considered special or memorable in the past.

December 6: Hold a family card-making party. Compile some pictures from throughout the year with captions. Then make color copies to include in your cards. Little ones can help apply address labels or stuff envelopes. Turn on some Christmas music and make this a fun time.

December 7: Plan a winter picnic. On a snowy day, prepare a lunch and warm drinks, pack everything into the car with some blankets, and set off for the park. Bundle up while you eat and have a blast playing in the snow. If you don't have snow where you live, plan an indoor picnic on the living room floor or in front of the fireplace.

December 8: Visit a nursing home as a family. Call ahead and find out how many residents live there. Take them inexpensive little gifts, homemade items, or fruit. Younger children can color some pictures to give away. Talk with the senior residents, and you just might make a few new friends. Join them in singing holiday carols or playing a game or two.

December 9: Organize a baking day. Invite friends or family over and bake all day long. Little ones can measure ingredients or have a table set up specifically for them to decorate cutout cookies. Freeze anything that can't be kept until Christmas. Pick a day to deliver these goodies to your friends and neighbors.

December 10: Go caroling! Join a group from your church or a local group, or gather a group of your friends and head out on your own. Sing in your neighborhood or go to some homes of elderly people and take them fruit baskets or handmade Christmas greetings. You don't need to have a voice like an angel to bring a smile to someone's face through song.

December 11: Pick a family that is in need. As a family, pray about ways you can help and decide how much money you will be spend to put together a gift package. Nonperishable groceries, school supplies, board games, and gift cards to grocery or clothing stores are great items to include. Plan an evening to deliver the package. Drive your entire family to the drop-off house and choose someone to make the delivery while you all watch from the car in a hidden parking spot. Place the package on the front porch in secret.

December 12: Go see *A Christmas Carol* or *The Nutcracker* at a local theater. Many high schools will present these or other plays and events for little or no cost. Check your local newspapers for dates and times. Invite grandparents and extended family to join you. If local drama doesn't interest your family, go see a Christmas movie at the movie theater.

December 13: Plan a family movie night. Take a trip to the video store and let everyone in your family pick out his or her favorite holiday movie. Serve pizza and popcorn. Break out the sleeping bags, pillows, and pajamas. This would also be a fun night to "camp out" under the Christmas tree and enjoy being together as a family.

December 14: Plan a game night with extended family and friends. Find some fun group games online and set out your favorite board games. Have some inexpensive prizes for the winners. To help keep the focus on the spirit of giving, ask guests to bring a nonperishable food item to donate to a local food bank as their entrance fee for game night.

December 15: Hold a letter-writing night. First take time to read through Psalm 139. Then write a letter to God telling Him how you feel about what He has to say in these verses. No one else needs to see this letter unless you want to share it. Then write a separate letter to each member of your family. Write something encouraging and tell them what you love about them. If you like, put these letters under the tree until Christmas Day, or share them as soon as you're finished writing.

December 16: If you have a long holiday road trip ahead of you, remember that there are plenty of fun activities to do as a family while you travel. Have one family member pick out several small games to bring along. Have another family member write down a list of questions—some serious, some ridiculous. Take turns asking each other these questions while you travel. Have another family member be in charge of picking out some yummy travel snacks.

December 17: Make family calendars to give away as gifts. Take pictures of each family member around the Christmas tree. Find some current school photos and take some new candids. Make sure each child has equal camera time. If you have a computer program that will make calendars for you, just scan your pictures and print. Or print out blank calendars and glue your pictures on the calendar for each month of the year. Make plenty of copies to give to grandmas, grandpas, and other special relatives or friends.

December 18: Take a lights tour! Pop some popcorn and gather some snacks and a thermos of hot cocoa. Drive to several neighborhoods and view Christmas lights after dark. Bundle up so you can see the lights with the car windows down. Bring your camera and take pictures of your favorite displays.

December 19: Let your animals enjoy the Christmas season, too. Decorate an animal-friendly tree in your yard just for the birds and squirrels living nearby. Adorn the tree with garland made of popcorn and berries. Roll pinecones in peanut butter and birdseed and hang on the tree.

December 20: Prepare for a relaxing evening at home. Eat dinner together and turn off the TV. Then bring out all the old family photo albums and relive some of the best memories you have made as a family. Take turns telling stories about the pictures and events. Then have everyone vote on the top five events in the life of your family so far.

December 21: Focus on the good news of great joy. Consider baking a birthday cake for Jesus or putting some candles on your favorite dessert or breakfast coffee cake. Don't forget to sing "Happy Birthday" to Him. Remember that we are celebrating the birth of Jesus all month long. Take turns having family members tell why Jesus birth is important and what it means to them today.

December 22: Make some room in your refrigerator for all of those wonderful Christmas desserts by having a smorgasbord night for dinner! Set out fruit, vegetables, dips, crackers, tortillas and any leftovers you would like to use up. Let the kids come up with their own creations. Cut food into bite-sized pieces and let everyone snack all evening long. Gather around the table and have fun showing each other your own recipes. Keep the snacks out to munch on while you play a game as a family.

December 23: Have each family member make and deliver special coupons to each other. Parents can make coupons for individual "date nights" with the kids. Spouses can make coupons for breakfast in bed or a foot massage. Children can make coupons for washing the dishes, cleaning the house, mowing the lawn, making the bed for a parent or sibling, and so forth. Each family member should receive at least one coupon from every member of your family in a decorated envelope.

December 24: Attend a candlelight Christmas Eve service with your family. If your church doesn't have a service by candlelight, look in the papers and call around to churches in your area. If you can't find one, hold a candlelight service at home. Light as many candles as you can find and sing some Christmas carols as a family. Don't forget to read the Christmas story from the Bible (found in Matthew 1 and Luke 2).

December 25: Have a grandparent or other family member take a picture of your immediate family. Turn this picture into an ornament and personalize it with your last name and the date. Make this a tradition each year. These personalized ornaments will be treasured as family heirlooms for years to come.

As you are opening and enjoying presents, eating fabulous food, and spending time with all of your family, don't forget to thank God for all that He has given you. If you wrote letters to each other for December 15's family activity, make time to read them today. Have a wonderful day as a family! Merry Christmas!

December 26: Spend some individual time with each family member today. Have breakfast with your daughter by the Christmas tree; have lunch with your son on a quilt in the living room; have dessert with your spouse in the kitchen; and so forth. Ask family members to tell you what they loved about Christmas this year. What were their favorite gifts? With whom did they have the best conversation over the holidays? What was it about? What was their favorite dessert? What was something new they'd never done before? What have they learned from Advent devotions?

December 27: Make it a point to have family night *at least* twice a month this coming year. Have family members take turns planning the activity and the menu. Even your youngest ones will have something to contribute. One time a month, have a surprise guest night. The event planner can invite one or two secret guests whom the whole family will enjoy having over—Grandma and Grandpa, a cousin, a Sunday school teacher, and so on. The rest of the family can take turns asking questions to try to guess who is coming.

December 28: God has given each of us spiritual gifts to share. Sit down as a family and try to figure out what each of your gifts are. Ask what your spouse and your kids feel passionate about. What are their strengths and weaknesses? Be honest with one another about this topic, and encourage each other in your gifts and talents. Discuss ways to get involved in your local church and missions.

December 29: Plan a family council night. Prepare your family's favorite meal and dessert. Let family members know ahead of time that they will be included in the discussion—everyone gets a say at family council! Ask questions such as the following: Are we spending enough time together as a family? Are we eating dinner together often enough throughout the week? What is important to each child? Talk about what each family member was thankful for this past year. Allow all members to share their goals for the coming year. Plan activities for your entire family to do in the next three months.

December 30: Plan a "take down the tree" party with your immediate family. Play festive music, have some refreshments handy, and start undecorating. Hang a special ornament in a hidden spot on your tree or in your house somewhere. As your family is cleaning up, the first one to find the special ornament gets a prize! You might even want to keep a few small gifts hidden under the tree for your children to find as they help take down the tree. This surprise makes a depressing job a lot more fun!

December 31: Plan a progressive dinner for New Year's Eve. Call up family and friends and decide which family will host the appetizer, the soup or salad, the main course, and the dessert. Drive to one home for the appetizer, another home for the soup or salad, and so on. This helps share the cost and responsibility of an otherwise expensive and large party. Watch the ball drop and ring in the new year at the last home!